Theory of Music Grade 1
November 2019

Your full name (as on appointment form). Please use BLOCK CAPITALS.

Your signature

Candidate number

Centre

Instructions to Candidates

1. The time allowed for answering this paper is **two (2) hours**.
2. Fill in your name and the candidate number printed on your appointment form in the appropriate spaces on this paper, and on any other sheets that you use.
3. **Do not open this paper until you are told to do so.**
4. This paper contains **six (6) sections** and you should answer all of them.
5. Read each question carefully before answering it. Your answers must be written legibly in pen or pencil in the spaces provided.
6. You are reminded that you are bound by the regulations for written exams displayed at the exam centre and listed on page 4 of the current edition of the written exams syllabus. In particular, you are reminded that you are not allowed to bring books, music or papers into the exam room. Bags must be left at the back of the room under the supervision of the invigilator.
7. If you leave the exam room you will not be allowed to return.

Examiner's use only:

1 (20)	
2 (20)	
3 (15)	
4 (15)	
5 (10)	
6 (20)	
Total	

(C-01)

November 2019 (C) — Grade 1

Section 1 (20 marks)

Put a tick (✓) in the box next to the correct answer.

Example

Name this note:

A ☐   D ☐   C ✓

This shows that you think **C** is the correct answer.

1.1 Name this note:

G ☐   A ☐   C ☐

1.2 Name this note:

F sharp ☐   D sharp ☐   D natural ☐

1.3 Name the notes to find the hidden word:

AGED ☐   CEDE ☐   CAGE ☐

1.4 How many crotchet beats are there in a dotted minim?   2 ☐   3 ☐   4 ☐

1.5 Add the total number of crotchet beats in these note and rest values:

= _____   5 ☐   6 ☐   7 ☐

November 2019 (C) — Grade 1

Put a tick (✓) in the box next to the correct answer.

1.6 Which rest matches the length of this note value?

1.7 Which is the correct time signature?

2/4 ☐   3/4 ☐   C ☐

1.8 To return the last note to the pitch of the first note, which accidental would you put just before it?

♮ ☐   ♯ ☐   ♭ ☐

1.9 Which pair of notes has a distance of a semitone between them?

G and A ☐   A and B flat ☐   B flat and C ☐

1.10 Which note is the tonic in the key of G major?

G ☐   C ☐   F ☐

1.11 Here is the scale of C major. Where are the semitones?

Between the 1st & 2nd and 3rd & 4th degrees ☐
Between the 3rd & 4th and 6th & 7th degrees ☐
Between the 3rd & 4th and 7th & 8th degrees ☐

1.12 Which major key has the following key signature?

G major ☐   F major ☐   C major ☐

November 2019 (C)   Grade 1

Put a tick (✓) in the box next to the correct answer.

1.13   Which chord symbol fits above this tonic triad?

       C ☐   F ☐   G ☐

1.14   Which note needs to be added to make a tonic triad in the key of F major?

       F ☐   A ☐   C ☐

1.15   Name this interval:

       3rd ☐   4th ☐   5th ☐

1.16   Name this interval:

       unison ☐   5th ☐   octave ☐

1.17   The bottom number of a time signature shows: the type of beats in a bar ☐
                                                                                  the number of beats in a bar ☐
                                                                                  what speed to play the music ☐

1.18   Dynamic markings tell a player: how loudly or softly to play ☐
                                       what speed to play the music ☐
                     how to play the notes (eg smoothly or with an accent) ☐

1.19   The following is:

       a scale going up ☐
       an arpeggio going up ☐
       an arpeggio going down ☐

1.20   What does **Andante** mean?   fast ☐
                                     soft ☐
                         at a walking pace ☐

November 2019 (C)   Grade 1

Section 2 (20 marks)

2.1 Write a one-octave G major scale in semibreves, going up. Use the correct key signature and mark the semitones with a bracket (∧ or ∨) and an **S** for semitone.

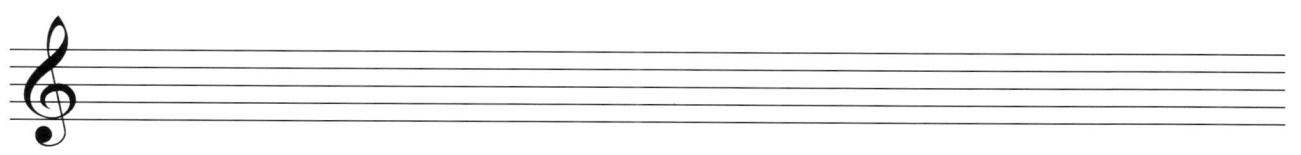

2.2 Write a one-octave F major arpeggio in semibreves, going up then down. Add the correct key signature.

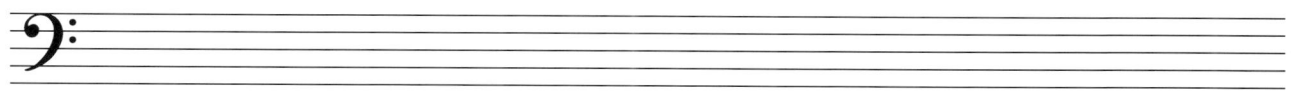

Section 3 (15 marks)

3.1 Circle five different mistakes in the following music, then write it out correctly.

(Please turn over for section 4)

November 2019 (C) Grade 1

Section 4 (15 marks)

4.1 Answer the following rhythm:

Section 5 (10 marks)

5.1 Here is an ostinato. Write two more repeats of the pattern.

November 2019 (C)　　　　　　　　　　　　　　　　　　　　　　　　　　　　　　　Grade 1

Section 6 (20 marks)

Look at the following piece and answer the questions below.

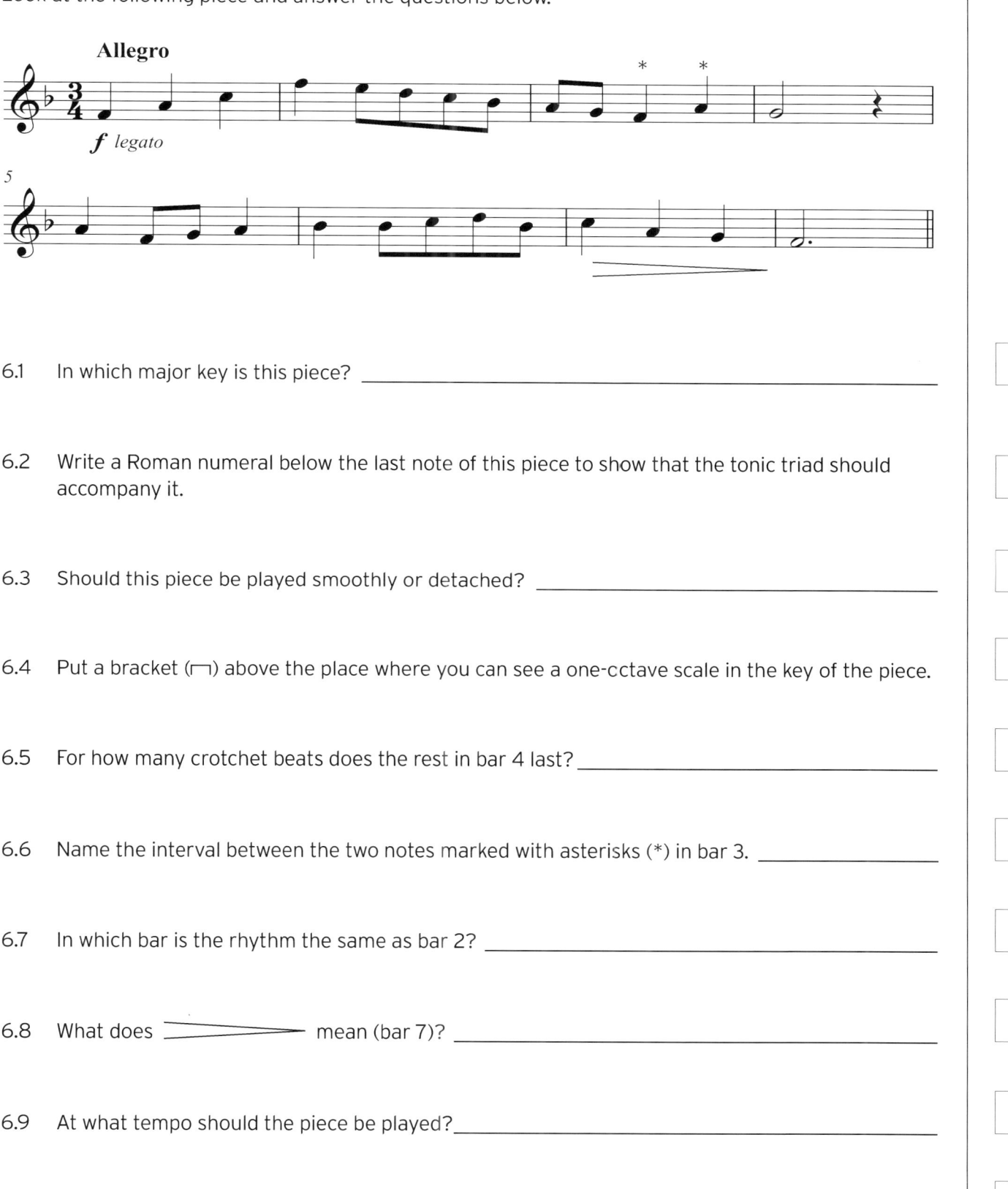

6.1　In which major key is this piece? _____

6.2　Write a Roman numeral below the last note of this piece to show that the tonic triad should accompany it.

6.3　Should this piece be played smoothly or detached? _____

6.4　Put a bracket (⊓) above the place where you can see a one-octave scale in the key of the piece.

6.5　For how many crotchet beats does the rest in bar 4 last? _____

6.6　Name the interval between the two notes marked with asterisks (*) in bar 3. _____

6.7　In which bar is the rhythm the same as bar 2? _____

6.8　What does ⟩ mean (bar 7)? _____

6.9　At what tempo should the piece be played? _____

6.10　**Doh** is written in two registers in this piece. Put a box (☐) around an example of a high and low **doh**.

Theory of Music Grade 1
November 2019

Your full name (as on appointment form). Please use BLOCK CAPITALS.

Your signature

Candidate number

Centre

Instructions to Candidates

1. The time allowed for answering this paper is **two (2) hours**.
2. Fill in your name and the candidate number printed on your appointment form in the appropriate spaces on this paper, and on any other sheets that you use.
3. **Do not open this paper until you are told to do so.**
4. This paper contains **six (6) sections** and you should answer all of them.
5. Read each question carefully before answering it. Your answers must be written legibly in pen or pencil in the spaces provided.
6. You are reminded that you are bound by the regulations for written exams displayed at the exam centre and listed on page 4 of the current edition of the written exams syllabus. In particular, you are reminded that you are not allowed to bring books, music or papers into the exam room. Bags must be left at the back of the room under the supervision of the invigilator.
7. If you leave the exam room you will not be allowed to return.

Examiner's use only:

1 (20)	
2 (20)	
3 (15)	
4 (15)	
5 (10)	
6 (20)	
Total	

(D-01)

November 2019 (D)   Grade 1

Section 1 (20 marks)

Put a tick (✓) in the box next to the correct answer.

Example

Name this note:

A ☐   D ☐   C ☑

This shows that you think **C** is the correct answer.

1.1   Name this note:

A ☐   middle C ☐   E ☐

1.2   Name this note:

F sharp ☐   D flat ☐   B flat ☐

1.3   Name the notes to find the hidden word:

CAGE ☐   CEDE ☐   CAFE ☐

1.4   How many crotchet beats are there in a semibreve?   2 ☐   3 ☐   4 ☐

1.5   Add the total number of crotchet beats in these note and rest values:

=   6 ☐   7 ☐   5 ☐

November 2019 (D)   Grade 1

Put a tick (✓) in the box next to the correct answer.

Boxes for examiner's use only

1.6   For how many crotchet beats does this rest last?

                                                          2 ☐   3 ☐   4 ☐

1.7   Which is the correct time signature?

                                                          $\frac{2}{4}$ ☐ $\frac{3}{4}$ ☐ $\frac{4}{4}$ ☐

1.8   To lower the pitch of this note by a semitone, which accidental would you put just before it?

                                                          ♯ ☐   ♮ ☐   ♭ ☐

1.9   Which pair of notes has a distance of a semitone between them?

                                       B and A ☐   F sharp and G ☐   D and C ☐

1.10   Which note is **doh** in the key of G major?   F ☐   C ☐   G ☐

1.11   Here is the scale of C major. Where are the semitones?

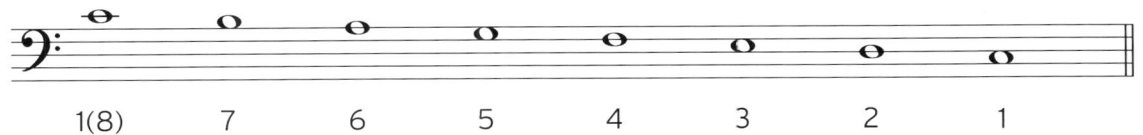

                                                                Between the 3rd & 4th and 5th & 6th degrees ☐
                                                                Between the 3rd & 4th and 7th & 8th degrees ☐
                                                                Between the 1st & 2nd and 5th & 6th degrees ☐

1.12   Which rest matches the length of this note?

                                                            ▬ ☐   𝄽 ☐   ▬ ☐

November 2019 (D) Grade 1

Put a tick (✓) in the box next to the correct answer.

1.13 Which major key has the following key signature?

F major ☐   C major ☐   G major ☐

1.14 Which chord symbol fits above this tonic triad?

C ☐   G ☐   F ☐

1.15 Which note needs to be added to make the tonic triad in the key of G major?

D ☐   G ☐   B ☐

1.16 Name this interval:

5th ☐   4th ☐   octave ☐

1.17 Name this interval:

2nd ☐   3rd ☐   unison ☐

1.18 What does **fortissimo** mean?

very loud ☐
loud ☐
getting gradually louder ☐

1.19 A tempo marking tells a player:

how softly or loudly to play ☐
what speed to play the music ☐
to play smoothly ☐

1.20 What does **staccato** mean?

play with an accent ☐
play smoothly ☐
play these notes short and crisp ☐

November 2019 (D)   Grade 1

Section 2 (20 marks)

2.1   Write a one-octave F major scale in semibreves, going up. Use the correct key signature and mark the semitones with a bracket (∧ or ∨) and an **S** for semitone.

2.2   Write a one-octave arpeggio of G major in semibreves, going down then up. Add the correct key signature.

Section 3 (15 marks)

3.1   Circle five different mistakes in the following music, then write it out correctly.

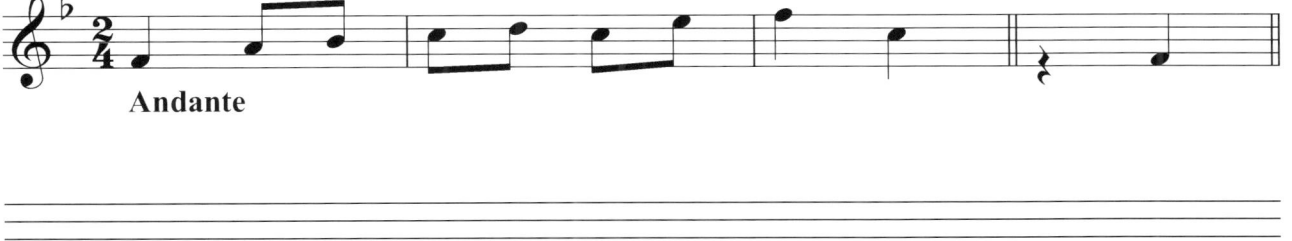

(Please turn over for section 4)

Section 4 (15 marks)

4.1 Answer the following rhythm:

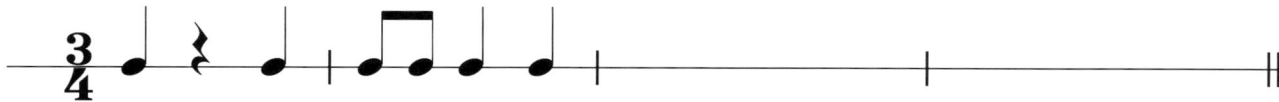

Section 5 (10 marks)

5.1 Here is an ostinato. Write two more repeats of the pattern.

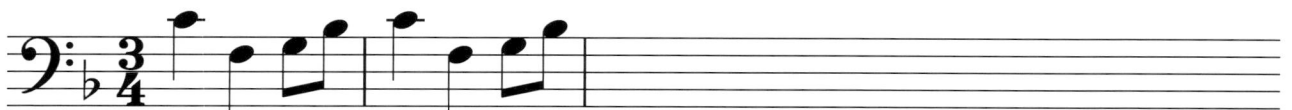

November 2019 (D)   Grade 1

Section 6 (20 marks)

Look at the following piece and answer the questions below.

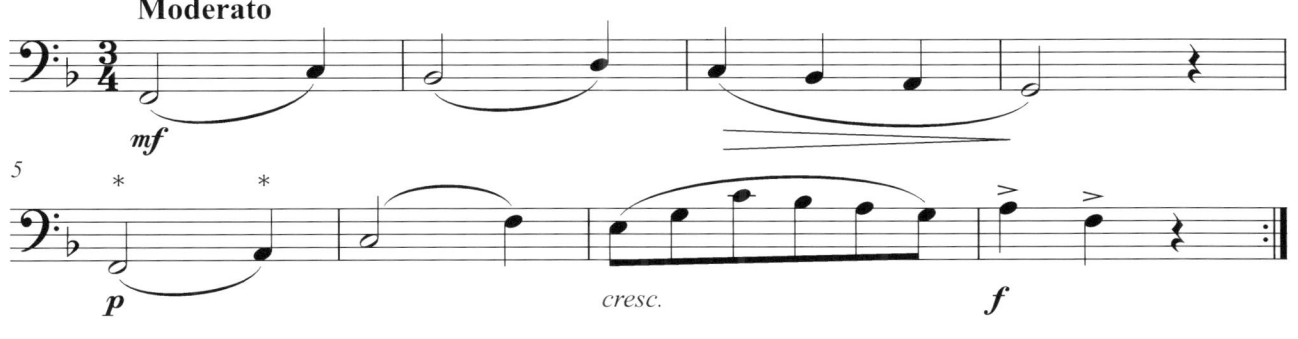

6.1   In which major key is this piece? _____

6.2   Write a Roman numeral below the last note of this piece to show that the tonic triad should accompany it.

6.3   The tonic note is written in two registers in this piece. Put a box (☐) around an example of a low and high tonic.

6.4   Put a bracket (⌐⌐) above a one-octave arpeggio in the key of the piece.

6.5   How many times does the rhythm 𝅗𝅥 𝅘𝅥 appear? _____

6.6   What does **Moderato** mean? _____

6.7   Name the interval between the two notes marked with asterisks (*) in bar 5. _____

6.8   For how many crotchet beats does the rest in bar 4 last? _____

6.9   What does *cresc.* mean? _____

6.10 Write the highest and lowest notes in this piece in crotchets.